Forces

Contents

Human strength	2
Pushing	4
In the playground	6
See-saws	8
Mobiles	9
Balancing toys	10
Bicycles	12
Poem	13
Spinning	14
Bouncing	15
The way we move	16
Old-fashioned toys	18
Two by two	20
Anders the toy-maker	
Glossary	24

Human strength

This man is in a competition to find the strongest man in the world. Imagine how much **force** he is using to lift this car.

This man is taking part in a tug-of-war. He is using a lot of force too. In a tug-of-war, each side tries to pull the other side towards them. The winners are the ones who pull the marker on the rope across the line.

Pushing

We all use force. Whenever we move something, we need to use some force. Sometimes we need to use a lot of force to move something.

When a car breaks down in the road, people need to push it out of the way of the rest of the traffic. It's very hard work.

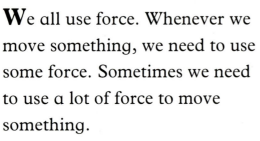

These elephants are very strong. Their strong trunks and bodies help them push hard enough to move the logs.

It's very hard work pushing your bicycle up a hill but it's easy coming down the other side!

Pushing a supermarket trolley needs a lot of force too, particularly if it's full of heavy shopping.

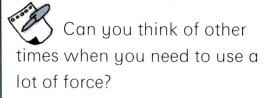

Can you think of other times when you need to use a lot of force?

In the playground

You need to use force to get the big toys in the playground working.

The harder you push on the roundabout, the faster it goes. You have to hold on tight so you don't get thrown off the edge. Spin-driers work in the same way. The wet clothes spin round and round very fast. The fast spinning forces the water to fly out of them.

You have to work hard to keep a swing going. After you have pushed off, you have to lean your body backwards and forwards to swing up high. When you stop working, the swing slows down. Your feet act as brakes and make the swing come to a complete stop.

Do you like going down the slide? You climb up the ladder, get into position and push off. You slide down the slippery slope quickly, but you slow down and stop at the bottom where it is flat.

A helter-skelter is like a slide. But it goes round and round and you can slide down very fast.

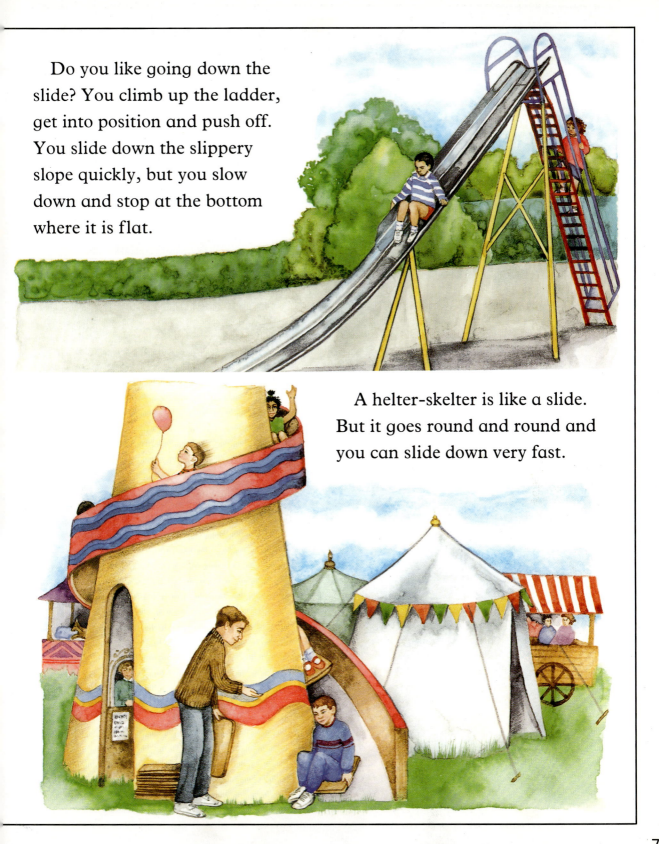

See-saws

See-saws are just like big **scales**. We balance both ends with our bodies. Pushes from our legs upset the balance and start us going up and down.

Have you ever played on a see-saw with your friends? If there is a see-saw nearby, try playing on it. Can you make it balance if you sit on one end and two other people sit on the other end? Can you make it balance with one person on one end and three people on the other end?

What if there is one person at each end and one person is heavier than the other?

Try making a model see-saw indoors. What can you use for the plank and the **pivot**? When you have made your see-saw, try balancing heavy and light objects on it.

Mobiles

This mobile is perfectly balanced. It slowly turns in a circle in the moving air. All the pieces are carefully balanced so that it doesn't get tangled up.

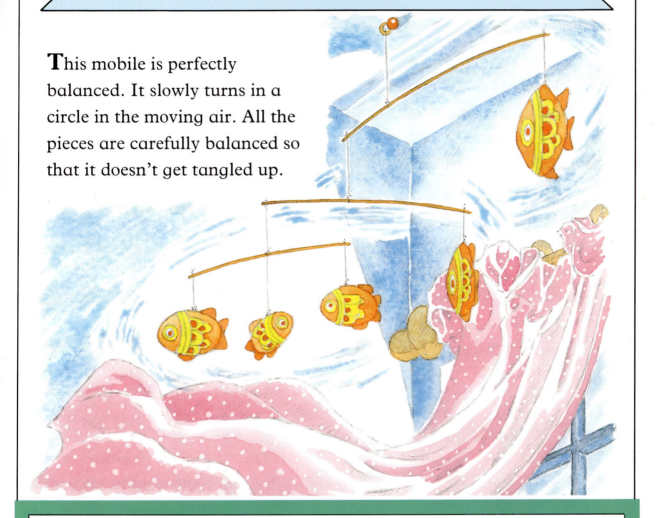

Can you make a mobile that has five things hanging from it? Try making one with a friend. You will need some thin sticks or plastic straws and some cotton or thin thread.

What do you want to hang from the mobile?

You can make shapes to hang from it, or you can hang objects that you have found, such as feathers or shells. You will need to make the mobile balance. It may take you several goes to make it balance properly.

Balancing toys

It is hard to keep your balance when you are standing on one foot. But you can use your arms and your free leg to help you balance so you don't fall over.

Many toys work by balancing. Kelly dolls keep their balance because they have nearly all their weight at the bottom. No matter how you knock them round, they always bounce back.

This parrot can sit on its perch all day. But if you take the weight off its tail, it will fall over. The bird uses a weight to keep it in position. If you push it, it will swing backwards and forwards. The weight on its tail helps to keep it balanced.

This baby doll balances on a pin-point. The weights on both sides keep it balanced.

Try making a double-decker bus out of an empty cereal box. Cut holes for windows. Can you make a floor for the upstairs part?

Does the bus balance well? Or does it fall over easily if you knock it?

See if it balances well with toy people sitting on the bottom floor. Does it balance well with people sitting on the top floor?

Can you invent a way to test when it falls over most easily? What can you do to the bus to make it balance better when there are people sitting upstairs but nobody sitting downstairs?

Charles Blondin walked across the Niagara Falls on a tightrope on 30th June 1859. The rope was 335 metres long and it was hung 49 metres above the falls.

About a year later he made the crossing again, but this time he carried a friend on his back!

Bicycles

You have to be able to keep your balance when you ride a bicycle. What happens if you lean over too far to the side when you are on your bike?

Can you think of any other times when you have to keep your balance? Are you good at balancing?

Esmé on her Brother's Bicycle

One foot on, one foot pushing, Esmé starting off beside
Wheels too tall to mount astride,
Swings the off leg forward featly,
Clears the high bar nimbly, neatly,
With a concentrated frown
Bears the upper pedal down
As the lower rises, then
Brings her whole weight round again,
Leaning forward, gripping tight,
With her knuckles showing white,
Down the road goes, fast and small,
Never sitting down at all.

Russell Hoban

Spinning

Some objects will keep their balance if you make them spin. A bicycle stays up while its wheels are spinning. It will fall over when they stop.

You can make a spinning-top work by spinning it between your fingers and thumb or by whipping a string around it. Can you make a coin spin on its side? How long can you keep it spinning for?

Yo-yos only work when they spin. As they unwind, they spin and get enough energy to wind up again and climb up the string. You have to keep spinning them to keep them going.

⭐ The person who has kept a yo-yo going for the longest time is an American called Bob Brown. He yo-yoed for 121 hours and ten minutes, from 24th to 28th June 1985! He did not have any sleep for five nights.

Bouncing

Most balls bounce back up after they are dropped. They lose some energy pushing against the air, so they get less high after each bounce. If you put lots of energy into your throw and throw a ball hard against the ground, it will shoot up higher than it started. The ball will keep on bouncing until the energy is used up.

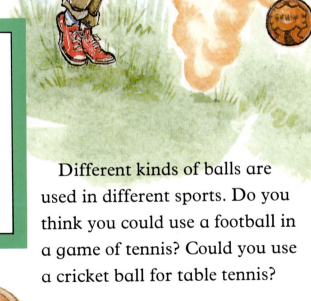

Do you think all balls bounce as high as each other? Make a collection of different balls. You will need ones of different sizes and different materials. Can you test them to see which bounces the highest?

Different kinds of balls are used in different sports. Do you think you could use a football in a game of tennis? Could you use a cricket ball for table tennis?

The way we move

How do you move? Can you hop, jump and run? Can you do a roll or a cartwheel? Think carefully about how you move. You use your legs and arms and your body to help balance, spin, bounce and jump.

Can you hop on one foot? How do you keep your balance? It is not always easy to balance on a narrow beam. Can you help yourself to balance? Do you do anything with your arms and legs to help you balance?

Can you do a roll or a cartwheel like this? You curl up into a ball when you do a roll. The ball shape helps you go round, head over heels. When you do a cartwheel you need to give yourself a big push to make the star shape go round. It's hard work!

Try jumping up in the air. First of all, try keeping your legs straight when you jump. Then try bending your knees when you jump. Which way helps you jump highest?

Is it easier to stop quickly when you are running or when you are walking? Can you think why?

Old-fashioned toys

Many toys are very simple but are still fun to play with. Some were invented a long time ago and used to be made at home.

This toy is sometimes called Peter and Paul. When you push and pull, the birds peck in turn from the food bowl. The simple wire hinges move the birds up and down.

A monkey on a stick can do all sorts of tricks. When you slide the bar up and down, the legs and arms of the puppet jump about.

Have you ever seen a pecking woodpecker? If you see it rocking on its spring, it will take a long time to stop. The collar holds it to the stick and the woodpecker slowly works to the bottom of the stick.

These waddling animals rock down a slope. Their weight makes them move from side to side. With each step, the legs on the other side fall forwards and take over.

The jack-in-the-box shoots out when you open the box. The spring is squashed inside until you open the lid. Then it jumps open.

Pogo sticks use springs too, to help you jump.

What is your favourite toy? Is it a model car or train, a spinning-top, a bicycle or a puppet? What do you think makes your favourite toys move?

Two by two

Anders was a toy-maker. He made dolls' houses, model soldiers and sets of wooden bricks for babies. Those were the toys people liked to buy. When Anders made other kinds of toys, no one bought them. They lay in his shop, gathering lots of dust.

I'm bored with soldiers, bricks and dolls' furniture. I wonder what else will sell?

One morning, when Anders was winding the clock after breakfast, he had an idea. He hurried round his workshop, gathering wood, glue, screws and paint. He fetched a leather belt from his bedroom. He took the clock to bits, and laid the motor carefully on the table in front of him.

When Anders had gathered everything, he set to work. He began by making a large toy ship. It had an opening in the side, with a door which went up and down like a drawbridge.

When the ship was finished Anders began carving wooden animals and birds. He made two chickens, two sheep, two pigs, two cows, two lions, two ostriches, two giraffes, two elephants, two doves, two dogs and two ravens. When each bird or animal was finished, he glued it to the leather belt. Soon the whole belt was covered. It looked as if the birds and animals were marching along in a line, two by two.

Next, Anders made two wooden cog-wheels, one big and one small. He fixed the big one inside the ship and fastened the small one to the clockwork motor from the clock. He made a wooden cover to hide the motor, and painted it green, like a grassy field.

Last of all, Anders fastened the leather belt round the cog-wheels, and sewed the ends to make a loop. Now it looked as if the line of animals was standing in a field, looking towards the ship.

At first the animals moved too quickly. Anders experimented with different sized cog-wheels until he got it right. Soon the new toy was ready. Anders wound up the motor and at once the cog-wheels began to turn.

They moved the belt along, and it looked as if the animals were marching through the field into the ship.

By now, crowds of people were gazing in at the window of Anders' shop.

Glossary

force
A force is needed to make something move. Pushes and pulls are simple forces.

pivot
The pivot is the point around which something turns. For example, a see-saw goes up and down on a pivot.

scales
Scales are used to balance or weigh objects.

Contents

What is an Island?................................3
Jamaica 6
Galápagos Islands 10
New Zealand 14
Prince Edward Island...........................18
Islands of the World 21
Glossary 23
Index 24

Los Roques Islands, Venezuela

What is an Island?

An island is a piece of land that is completely surrounded by water. Islands are found all over the world. Each has its own **climate**. Jamaica is warm and sunny with sandy beaches and palm trees. Greenland is very cold. It is covered with ice and snow for most of the year. New Zealand has warm and cold climates in different places.

The city of Hobart is on the island state of Tasmania, which lies off the south coast of **mainland** Australia.

Islands are home to many types of plants and animals. A few islands have their own **wildlife** that is not found anywhere else in the world. This is because the islands are separated from other land by sea or ocean.

Lemurs are found only on the island of Madagascar.

The largest island is Greenland. One of the smallest islands is Bishop Rock. It only has room for a lighthouse.

Ilulissat, Greenland

Bishop Rock, England

Many people living on large islands have their own language and **culture**. They usually find work in the towns and cities on the island.

On small islands a few people might work in **tourism** on the island. But more people travel to the **mainland** to work. If not enough food is produced on the island, then they will buy that on the mainland, too.

This map shows the islands you can read about in this book.

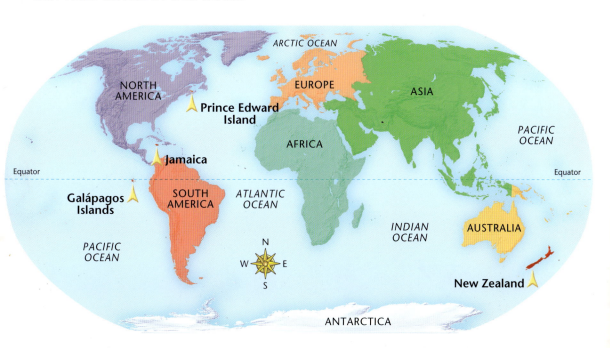

Jamaica

Tourists from many different countries visit Jamaica. It is found in the Caribbean Sea, off the coast of Central America. Jamaica has a warm **climate** and beautiful landscape. There are **rainforests**, rivers, waterfalls and white beaches.

Jamaica is famous for its Blue Mountains. In fact, Jamaica was formed from the tops of undersea mountains.

FACT FILE

Jamaica

Kingston

Caribbean Sea

Capital: Kingston

Area: 10,991 square km

Population: about 2.6 million people

Official Language: English

Currency: Jamaican dollar

Jamaica's Blue Mountains

Jamaican guavas and pineapples are shipped to many countries.

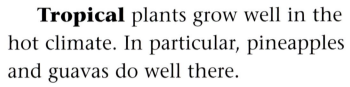

Tropical plants grow well in the hot climate. In particular, pineapples and guavas do well there.

There are at least 200 different types of birds on the island. These include parakeets and pelicans. Bats, crocodiles, lizards, frogs, rats and mongooses live there, too.

The streamertail bird is found only in Jamaica.

Over thousands of years many different groups of people have lived in Jamaica. Today Jamaican **culture** is a combination of several different cultures. Most people have African ancestors. This has influenced Jamaican music. Today steel drum bands, calypso, ska and reggae are popular in Jamaica.

Reggae Music
Reggae is a style of music invented in Jamaica in the late 1960s. It has a strong, four-beat rhythm. The rhythm is produced by the drums, bass guitar, electric guitar and scraper.

Musicians play the steel drums.

Jamaica's **tropical climate** allows people to grow many crops throughout the year. Islanders grow and sell sugar, bananas, coffee and cocoa. Many islanders make a living by fishing in the Caribbean Sea. Others mine for bauxite (BAWK-site). This is used to make aluminium. **Tourism** provides jobs on the island, too.

Coffee is grown in the Blue Mountain region in eastern Jamaica.

Fruit and vegetables grown on the island are sold in street markets.

Galápagos Islands

The Galápagos Islands are found in the Pacific Ocean, about 1000 kilometres west of **mainland** Ecuador.

Places near the **equator** are usually hot and wet. But the Galápagos Islands are cool and dry. This is because seawater drifts up from icy Antarctica and cools the land.

The Galápagos Islands were formed from underwater volcanoes along the equator.

Thirteen main islands and six small islands make up the Galápagos.

FACT FILE

Galápagos Islands

PACIFIC OCEAN

Provincial Capital: Puerto Baquerizo Moreno

Area: 7,882 square km (all islands together)

Population: about 18,000 people

Official Language: Spanish

Currency: US dollar

It is illegal to capture or remove giant tortoises or their eggs.

Some animals are found only on the Galápagos Islands. These include the giant tortoise and the fur seal. The giant tortoise grows to 1.5 metres long and weighs about 150 kilograms. It lives for about 150 years.

A fur seal grows to 1.5 metres long and weighs about 60 kilograms. People used to hunt it for its beautiful fur. Now this is illegal.

fur seal

In 1959 Ecuador made the Galápagos Islands a national park to protect the **wildlife**. Today tourists from around the world come to see the rare animals. Tour groups are kept small to protect the special plants and animals. Visitors are not allowed to touch them or get close to their nests.

A tourist photographs two blue-footed boobies.

Science of Survival
Charles Darwin (1809–1882) visited the Galápagos Islands in 1835. He realised that the wildlife on the islands was unique. He wrote a book that explained how these plants and animals had changed over time to survive.

Puerto Baquerizo Moreno is on the island of San Cristóbal.

Few people live on the Galápagos Islands because the land is protected. Hotels and cities are not allowed to be built there. Most people who live on the island work in **tourism** or grow crops including sugar and coffee. Scientists stay on the islands for a while to study the wildlife. Then they return home to write about their discoveries.

marine iguanas

New Zealand

New Zealand is found to the south of the **equator**. It has two main islands: the North Island and the South Island.

New Zealand is famous for its beautiful green landscape. There are **rainforests**, beaches, mountains, volcanoes and **fjords**. On the North Island there are volcanic hot springs and **geysers**.

FACT FILE

New Zealand

Capital: Wellington

Area: 270,534 square km

Population: about 4 million people

Official Language: English

Currency: New Zealand dollar

Pohutu Geyser, North Island

The Southern Alps are on the South Island.

New Zealand's **climate** varies from north to south. It is almost **tropical** at the northern tip of the North Island. Yet it is very cold at the southern tip of the South Island.

Many types of plants and animals live in these different climates. Some animals are found only in New Zealand. These include the saddleback bird and the kiwi bird.

kiwi bird

kiwi fruit

New Zealand has different types of forests which include many rare trees and plants. The kauri (KOW-ree) pine is found in ancient forests. It is one of the largest trees in New Zealand. Beech trees and giant tree ferns are also found in the forests.

◄ Kauri trees can grow to more than 50 metres tall.

▲ This silver fern, or ponga tree, is a national symbol of New Zealand.

The first people to live on the islands were the Maori (MOW-ree). Today many people's families originally came from Britain.

There are many more farm animals than people in New Zealand. Sheep and cattle graze in the grassy fields. New Zealand sells meat, dairy products and wool to other countries. Most people live in towns and cities.

Maori Welcome
The Maori have a special greeting called the Hongi. They press their foreheads and noses together to express friendship.

Auckland is a city on the North Island.

Prince Edward Island

Prince Edward Island is found on Canada's east coast in the Gulf of St Lawrence.

Viewed from the air, the island looks like a colourful patchwork quilt. In reality the quilt squares are crops growing in the soil. The **fertile** red soil is good for growing potatoes, turnips, grain and blueberries.

FACT FILE

Capital: Charlottetown

Area: 5,660 square km

Population: about 139,900 people

Official Language: English

Currency: Canadian dollar

fields on Prince Edward Island

Brackley Beach is a popular place for holiday makers.

Prince Edward Island has cold winters and cool springs. It is very popular with tourists who visit its sand dunes and beaches.

More than 300 species of birds live on the island. These include great blue herons, piping plovers and bald eagles. Red squirrels, snowshoe hares, red foxes, minks, beavers and muskrats live there, too.

a rare piping plover

Prince Edward Island has rich, **fertile** soil, which is perfect for farming. As a result, many islanders earn a living from farming. They grow potatoes, turnips, hay and grain to sell abroad. A few islanders grow trees and sell the timber. Others go fishing along the coast for cod, lobster, mackerel and tuna.

Fishing boats line a harbour.

Lobsters are caught off the coast.

Canada's Birthplace

Charlottetown is the capital of Prince Edward Island. It is known as Canada's birthplace. In 1864 the first of several important meetings were held here. These meetings led to the formation of Canada as we know it today.

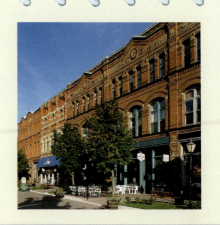

Islands of the World

Jamaica, the Galápagos Islands, New Zealand and Prince Edward Island are all unique islands. They have their own **climates** and **wildlife**. Here are some more unique islands from around the world.

Greenland is found in the northern Atlantic Ocean. Most of it is covered in ice. For a few weeks in the summer, there is no night. In winter, there is no daylight. Greenland is the largest island in the world.

The **Maldives** are found in the Indian Ocean. They are made up of about 1,200 tiny coral islands. Sandy beaches, lagoons and coconut palms cover them. The islands were once underwater volcanoes.

Madagascar is found in the Indian Ocean. Rainforests cover the island and provide a home for lemurs, chameleons and geckoes. It is the world's fourth largest island.

Great Britain is found in the Atlantic Ocean and North Sea. It is made up of England, Scotland and Wales. Great Britain is separated from Ireland by the Irish Sea and from France by the English Channel.

Japan is found in the Pacific Ocean. It is made up of four large islands and more than 1,000 smaller islands. Japan has high mountains and lush green fields. Tokyo is the capital city and one of the largest cities in the world.

Glossary

climate   the pattern of weather in a place over time

culture   the customs and practices of a group of people

equator   an imaginary line around the middle of the Earth, dividing the northern and southern hemispheres

fertile   capable of producing many crops

fjords   deep, narrow waterways between steep cliffs formed by glaciers

geysers   underground springs that shoot boiling water and steam out of the ground

mainland   the main part of a country, which may have islands around its coast

rainforest   tropical forest with high rainfall

tourism   the business of providing services to people who are on holiday

tropical   found in the warm area near the equator

wildlife   wild animals and plants

Index

Canada 18, 20
climate 3, 6, 7, 9, 15, 21
crops 9, 13, 18
culture 5, 8
Darwin, Charles 12
Ecuador 10, 12
equator 5, 10, 14
farming 20
fishing 9, 20
fjords 14
forests 16
fur seal 11
Galápagos Islands
    10–13, 21
geysers 14
giant tortoise 11
Great Britain 22
Greenland 3, 4, 21
Hawaii 24
Jamaica 3, 5, 6–9, 21
Japan 22
kauri pine 16
kiwi bird 15
Madagascar 4, 22
Maldives 21

Maori 17
mining 9
New Zealand 3, 14–17, 21
Prince Edward Island
    18–20, 21
rainforests 6, 14, 22
reggae music 8
saddleback bird 15
tourism 5, 9, 13
tourists 6, 12, 19
volcanoes 10, 14, 21
wildlife 4, 12, 13, 21

Panalu'u Beach Park, Big Island, Hawaii